THE BOOK PROPOSAL

7 Easy Steps to Writing a Successful Book Proposal

by

Kathy Bruins

and

Kim de Blecourt

Printed in the United States of America

First Edition

ISBN-13: 978-1514276549

ISBN-10: 1514276542

Scripture quotations marked "KJV" are taken from the Holy Bible, King James Version, Cambridge, 1769.

Scripture quotations marked "NIV" are taken from HOLY BIBLE, NEW INTERNATIONAL VERSION. Copyright 1973, 1978, 1984 by International Bible Society. Used by permission of Zondervan Publishing House.

Scripture quotations marked "TLB" or "The Living Bible" are taken from The Living Bible [computer file] / Kenneth N. Taylor. electronic ed. Wheaton : Tyndale House, 1997, c1971 by Tyndale House Publishers, Inc. Used by permission. All rights reserved.

Scripture taken from *The Message*. Copyright © 1993, 1994, 1995, 1996, 2000, 2001, 2002. Used by permission of NavPress Publishing Group.

Endorsements

A few years ago, as the directors of the Florida Christian Writers Conference, we asked Kathy Bruins and Kim de Blecourt to join our faculty in a pre-conference workshop that would teach our conferees what they needed to know about writing book proposals. Kathy and Kim immediately told us that our conferees would not only know *how,* they would walk out *with* a book proposal, ready to show the agents and editors they hoped to impress. That first year, we held our collective breath, waiting to hear the reaction of the conferees who had opted for the class. For the remainder of the conference we heard the same thing: "If I'd only gotten to the book proposal workshop, it would have been enough!" The following year Kathy and Kim returned and the results were the same ... and the next year and so on and so forth. We cannot *imagine* our conference without Kathy and Kim's book proposal studio, and we highly recommend what they offer within these pages.

Eva Marie Everson
Mark Hancock
Directors
Florida Christian Writers Conference

Testimonials from The Book Proposal Studio
Taught by Kathy Bruins and Kim de Blecourt

"I came to the conference and workshop feeling unfocused, confused, and lacking confidence. I took my notes back to my room and worked on a proposal/pitch and found the clarity and organization for my thoughts that enabled me to make presentations on two separate projects that resulted in three different editors asking me to submit my work. This workshop is worth its weight in gold. The time and care Kathy and Kim take with the students is phenomenal. If you're looking for a star rating—I give them the most. My best advice: don't miss the opportunity to take the class or buy the book!"—Tina M. Hunt, Speaker, Writer, Consultant

"The Book Proposal (Studio) has an easy-to-follow format that helped me create a concise one-sheet and a ready-to-go look for my book proposal!"—Brenda S. Gibson, Author

"Kathy and Kim provide excellent guidance for compiling one-sheets and book proposals, along with practical tips and samples."—Remi Oyedele, Author

"I loved your class. I hadn't been to a writers' conference in three years, and I didn't realize they were doing the one-page. I ran back to my room that evening, made a one-page, and gave it to agents I had appointments with. I had three agents ask me to send them a proposal. I can't thank you enough for showing me the one-page."—Marie Bast, Author

"The two things I appreciated the most were the clear way the book proposal was organized and the hands-on help, reading my one-sheet, giving feedback, letting me know what was missing, what could add punch, etc."—Roberta Fish, Author

"Thank you for all your insight and help in your class on book proposals and the one-page. Since arriving home from the conference, I have been diligently writing, editing, and rewriting."—William Castaldi, Author

"As Christian authors, we all have an important message. I want to share a message of hope to those who have been devastated by divorce. I met with several agents and publishers and got some good feedback. Several asked for a proposal. Thank you for your encouragement."—Cary Sanchez, Licensed Clinical Social Worker

To God, who makes all things possible, I give Him praise!

To all the scribes who have gone before me, taught me, and left a legacy for me, you have inspired me to turn and give back to those following me.
With much appreciation,
Kathy

For my gracious heavenly Father, loving husband, Jahn, our daughter, Jacey, and son, Jake. You make my life story complete with your love, understanding, and support.
All my love,
Kim

A special thank you to Kathy Ide for the wonderful help she gave this book with her expert editing skills. She brought the work to another level and we appreciate it very much.

INTRODUCTION

"That I may publish with the voice of thanksgiving, and tell of all thy wondrous works." Psalm 26:7 KJV

Congratulations! You have entered the professional world of writing. Whether it is a great book idea in your mind or a completed manuscript in your hands, you have reached the point in your author journey where you need to communicate like a professional. Regardless of your writing dreams, learning the industry is no longer suggested, it is required.

The world of literary agents and book publishing uses its own terminology and expected documentation. This book focuses on your biggest introduction to the world of agents and editors—your book proposal.

A book proposal is the accepted format to present your fiction or nonfiction book idea to an agent or acquisitions editor for a traditional publishing house. Even with a completed manuscript, the book proposal is the only accepted documentation among literary professionals. This important tool helps you be perceived as the professional you are or hope to become.

The book proposal also enables you to view your book in total, in advance of its completion. Many authors utilize their book proposals as a planning tool before their writing process begins.

Book proposals should be requested, not submitted. So how do you receive a request? Completing a one-sheet or sending a query letter are a couple of ways to present your idea. Therefore, instructions for these are also included in this book.

As the name suggests, the one-sheet reflects concisely, in a single page, the information of your book proposal, and it is presented to agents and editors at writers' conferences. Writers' conferences provide the best way for you to meet potential agents or publishers. If they like what they read in your one-sheet, they will most likely invite you to submit a book proposal.

Perhaps the agent or publisher you desire to meet isn't attending any writers' conferences this year. A query letter will communicate your desire for that person to review your manuscript. A well-written query letter can get you an invitation to send your book proposal for an agent's or editor's consideration. Instructions regarding how to create and use a query letter are included in this book.

You will also find a template to help you create your book proposal in a professional format that will impress acquisitions editors and literary agents. You can type your information right into the template.

The book proposal, the book one-sheet, and the query letter are all tools that, once learned, will enable you to enter the book publishing world in a professional manner.

Welcome to your role as an author in the publishing world!

THE HOOK

"Trust God from the bottom of your heart; don't try to figure out everything on your own. Listen for God's voice in everything you do, everywhere you go; he's the one who will keep you on track."
Proverbs 3:5–6 MSG

Have you ever received an invitation in the mail to attend a wedding? It looks fancy. A lot of work and thought went into it giving you the message that they want you to attend, which makes you feel valued.

The Hook of a book proposal can do the same thing for an editor. It's basically a title page that allows the acquisitions editor to view your idea as an actual book. Although there is nothing fancy about it, this important first page has a lot of white space, inviting tired eyes to embark on the journey of your proposal.

The format of your title page should be as follows:

- Two inches from the top of the page, type the title of the book in all caps. Capital letters make the title memorable.

- On the next line, type the subtitle in normal title format which is upper and lower case. Only nonfiction manuscripts have subtitles.
- Skip a line and then type "Submitted by"
- On the next line, type your name the way you want it to appear on the book.
- Skip a couple of lines and enter your contact information (each segment on a separate line): name (your real name, not a pseudonym), mailing address, phone number (cell and home), and e-mail address. This will make it easy for the editor or agent to contact you to discuss your book.
- Skip a line and then type your one-sentence pitch. This is what will grab the agent's or editor's attention.
- Skip a line, type a testimony from a well-known person or expert in the field, if you have one.
- Skip a line and then type your back-cover sales copy.

General formatting guidelines for your book proposal are as follows:
- Use Times New Roman font, twelve-point size, and do not right-justify the lines.
- Number the pages using a running header beginning with the page following the title page including sample chapters.
- Not including the title page, single-space all the lines

except the sample chapters, which need to be double-spaced.

THE PITCH

When a baseball player pitches to a batter, he is giving that player the option to either hit the ball or let it go by. Sometimes the batter hits a home run. Other times they strike out. Acquisitions editors and agents also discern from the pitch whether they should let a book go by or swing at it for a possible home run.

The pitch identifies a need readers have and proposes a solution: your book. Like the back cover of a paperback, your pitch has to be concise—only two or three sentences. Just explain the basic concept, like a thesis statement.

Explain the needs you are addressing and the solutions offered in your book.(Example: In my book, you will learn how to stop snoring by using essential oils.) Stick to the facts without stretching or exaggerating the truth.

If you're having trouble creating a pitch, compare your proposed book to similar published books, such as: "(Your book title) is like (a similar book title) meets (another similar book title)." The books you compare yours to should be instantly recognizable.

Memorize your pitch in case you need it at a moment's notice. If an agent or editor happens to be standing next to you in an elevator and asks about your book, you don't want to trip over your words. That would communicate a lack of professionalism.

BACK-COVER COPY

Your one- or two-sentence pitch acts as a great starting point; however, interested publishers will want to know more. Think of your expanded pitch as your book's back-cover copy. Most people read the summary on the back of a book before deciding to purchase it. Your expanded pitch functions as a sales tool from you to the publisher, and later from the publisher to your potential readers. Your back-cover copy lengthens your "elevator pitch" from one or two sentences to one or two paragraphs. Write this short summary of the main story line with exciting words that communicate, "You've got to read this!" Visit a bookstore or library and read the back-cover copy of several books in your genre. Which ones made you want to read those books? Refer to them when you write your sales copy.

An example of a hook and back-cover copy follows on the next page.

Until We All Come Home

A TRUE STORY OF ONE WOMAN'S COMMITMENT TO THE SON SHE REFUSED TO LEAVE BEHIND

Submitted by

Kim de Blecourt

Contact information: 123 Main St., City, State, Zip
(123) 456-7899
Kim123@gmail.com

One woman's battle against a corrupt government
to save her son and their race for freedom.

"I learned something powerful in hearing this story. Never, ever, never, never, never, never, ever, EVER mess with Kim and Jahn de Blecourt's family. An amazing story you will not easily forget." —Glynn Washington, host of "Snap Judgment," National Public Radio

Example of Sales Copy [should be formatted the same as "Hook" example above] In a story echoing the drama of *Not without My Daughter,* the intrigue of *The Hunt for Red October,* and the faith of *The Hiding Place, Until We All Come Home* recounts the journey of Kim de Blecourt, an American mother forced to navigate the corrupt post-Soviet political underworld in order to extricate her adopted son from an unscrupulous judicial system as they race for freedom just steps ahead of authorities.

A three-year-old boy struggles to survive in a Ukrainian orphanage. An American family senses God's call to adopt a child from a foreign land. What unfolds is a spellbinding true-life story of commitment, sacrifice, and intrigue as a mother single-handedly takes on a corrupt foreign legal system and lives in hiding for nearly a year as she pieces together the plan that will hopefully free her from impending arrest and bring her son home to freedom.

THE SLANT

"We should make plans—counting on God to direct us."
Proverbs 16:9 TLB

Communicating how your book is unique to a prospective editor or agent will improve its marketability. This chapter introduces the three areas publishers want to know about your book idea.

UNIQUE ANGLE

Use three to six bullet points to show how your book differentiates from others. Start each one with an action verb such as exceeded, maximized, captivated, etc.

CURRENT INTEREST

Is your book's topic of interest today? Are others writing about it? What statistics back up the interest level in your proposed book? What national organization promotes this interest?

MANUSCRIPT DETAILS

In this section, specify the current word count, anticipated completion date, and any special features.

The word count communicates to the editor or agent the length of your book. Generally, each chapter should run approximately 2,500 words. Novels and nonfiction should run from 50,000 to 110,000 words. Novellas should be 20,000 to 50,000 words. It's important to use a round number to communicate the word count.

The completion date of the manuscript informs the publisher when to schedule the printing. The standard time to complete a manuscript is six, nine, or twelve months after acceptance of a proposal. (When you do sign a contract, make sure to finish the manuscript on time.)

Special Features indicate what graphs, photos, tables, charts, or illustrations the publisher can expect for your book. The price of producing the book with these special features will be evaluated. If you have a lot of them that may add quite a bit to the printing bill and may discourage the publisher from accepting the manuscript as submitted.

An example of these features is shown on the next three pages.

PURPOSE

Humanity's deepest desire is to be known and loved. *Until We All Come Home* touches that deep human need through the power of a gripping story—the true story of Kim de Blecourt, a woman relentlessly pursuing an abandoned child. A woman willing to take on a post-Soviet government system and face threat of arrest, imprisonment, and even death, for the sake of love.

Until We All Come Home resonates with both male and female readers because it is a story of persevering love and courage, complete with the plot twists and turns similar to *The Bourne Identity*. Like biblical characters of old—David standing against Goliath and Esther standing before King Ahasuerus—the protagonist takes on an antagonist of epic proportions and faces seemingly insurmountable, life-threatening obstacles, while relying on faith in God to provide for her needs in every crisis. Readers will be drawn into the author's struggle with universal questions: What is our responsibility to a suffering world? How do we recognize the voice of God when we feel called to move forward into places of risk, especially when those choices may seem to defy common sense? How are we to respond when the price of love comes at a high cost? How will we react when we are confronted with our greatest fears?

Through the well-crafted unfolding of its true story, *Until We All Come Home* provides readers with insights into life's most challenging questions. Readers battle with the author as she stands alone against a corrupt adoption system in a post-Soviet country and battles to free her son, fleeing authorities as she faces threats of arrest and imprisonment.

Books by Russell D. Moore, Tom David, et al., note the growing American trend toward adoption, especially within the church. Few books, however, portray the detailed struggles of adoptive parents. One of the most important titles, *Adopted for Life* by Russell D. Moore (Crossway Book, 2009), offers brilliant reasoning for why it is so important for the church to be involved in adoption, but it does not offer readers an intimate, inspirational story of faith set against the backdrop of suspense and international intrigue that can shape the sometimes difficult international adoption journey.

This book is written in the popular memoir/travel style of *Eat, Pray, Love* and *Not Without My Daughter*. The book's message is inspirational and entertaining, with its interweaving of suspense and drama, set against a rich backdrop of information about international culture, the post-Soviet government system, and the changing face of adoption in some Eastern European nations.

UNIQUE ANGLE

In this book, the author:

- Recounts her courageous journey, spanning almost one year living in Ukraine, when she was forced to hide as a criminal and flee to secure the freedom of her newly adopted son in the country that granted custody to her family, then refused to allow him to leave.
- Takes the reader deep into the often-corrupt world of international adoption.
- Presents the unique differences between the author's Western culture and the post-Soviet, Ukrainian culture within the context of a compelling story.
- Offers the reader hope as the author relates true-life situations where God's miraculous intervention is evident. Shares her personal despair in moments of crisis and abandonment and how her faith provided not only a foundation for survival but the hope that brought her home.

CURRENT INTEREST

Adoption stories are currently receiving increased attention in the media. Spanning news broadcasts regarding the need of Haiti's orphans to celebrity international adoptions, adoption interest reflects an all-time high. Orphan and adoption themes have even been the subject of award-winning films, including *Slumdog*

Millionaire and *The Blind Side.*

The National Data Analysis System report shows a 180 percent increase in the number of international adoptions over the past sixteen years.

Due to the influence of such religious organizations as the Christian Alliance for Orphans and support for the orphan cause by Christian entertainers such as Steven Curtis Chapman, the popularity of adoption in Christian circles and the church's involvement in adoption is also trending.

Memoirs featuring strong female characters are also a popular trend. This is especially evident in recent successful books such as *Eat, Pray, Love* by Elizabeth Gilbert (Viking Adult, February 2006).

Until We All Come Home's combination of a suspense-filled international story with a strong female protagonist driven by a commitment to love packs a compelling one-two punch in today's competitive market.

MANUSCRIPT DETAILS

Word Count: 55,500
Completion Date: Four to six months after a signed contract
No Special Features

THE AUDIENCE

"It is God himself who has made us what we are and given us new lives from Christ Jesus; and long ages ago he planned that we should spend these lives in helping others." Ephesians 2:10 TLB

PURPOSE

To whom are you writing your book? What basic human need is being explored and met by your manuscript? Knowing your audience is important as you write and market your manuscript.

To fully understand your book's purpose, explore:

- Who will resonate with your book's topic?
- What biblical references, stories, or themes does your book touch on?
- What popular topic does your book bring up?
- Why is your book's message important?
- What question(s) does your book answer?

Address each of these questions in this section of your proposal. Conclude by summarizing the ultimate message of your book.

WHO IS YOUR AUDIENCE?

Define its characteristics, motivations, and interests. Understanding these will help you know more about the audience to whom you're writing. Write what you know about the audience of your book on the proposal.

Characteristics include age range, gender, stage in life, personal experience, and many other factors. One resource you may want to use is www.statista.com or google "statistics" and the topic in which you are looking.

Motivations are what makes this audience want to read your book. Do they want to lose weight, be a better parent, etc. Their need for a solution to their dilemma, or their desire to connect with someone who's had a similar experience, drives their desire to purchase your book.

Interest groups include gatherings of people (in person or online) who are attracted to the same subject, such as Mothers of Preschoolers (MOPS), American Cancer Society, and others. Subject interest, like human trafficking or Bible study, would draw them to your book if they're interested in that same theme.

Pinpointing your audience will help you write to readers more specifically. It's like trying to sell an idea to someone you know instead of to a stranger. Once you have some background information on them, you can choose words in which they will agree. You want your book to speak to the people for whom it is intended.

READER BENEFITS

What take-away will the readers' experience? Will reading your book change their lives, teach them, or inspire them?

Why would someone seek out your book? Start with a header sentence, such as:

If mothers of preschoolers read [*Title of your book*], they will:

Then use bullet points to list five to seven reader benefits. These can be the main points of your book (for nonfiction) or the obstacles your hero or heroine overcomes (for fiction). Each point should be concise and direct.

Begin each reader benefit with a verb, such as:

- Be inspired to …
- Grow in …
- Witness …
- Be educated in …
- Think differently about …

Listing Reader Benefits will improve your ability to sell

your book to the right market.

An example for the Audience Section follows on the next two pages.

AUDIENCE

The 14.8 million American readers who purchased travel books in 2007 reflected an increase of 11 percent from 2005. People today want to read books with a suspense angle and/or a strong female protagonist, such as *Eat, Pray, Love.*

The 80 million American adults who have committed their lives to Jesus Christ find encouragement in dynamic true stories of faith.

The 2 million American adults who annually consider adoption.

READER BENEFIT

- Readers will be inspired by this true story of relentless faith in the face of seemingly insurmountable conflict, hardship, and danger.
- Readers will identify with the author's sense of abandonment and eventual resolve in the face of eroding support from friends at home who believe it is impossible for an American mother to single-handedly free her adopted son from an unbending and unscrupulous Ukrainian judicial system.
- Readers will grow in their own journeys of faith watching the author wrestle with life-threatening circumstances as she leans into the sufficiency of God.
- Readers will witness the miraculous intervention of God as He provides protection, provision, and means of escape at precise moments, each time moving the author one step closer to the goal of freedom for herself and her son.
- Readers will learn about the political complexities of international adoption.
- Readers will gain insight into the challenges faced by Americans navigating Eastern European cultures.

- Readers will be educated regarding issues related to the realities of international orphan ministry and the global orphan crisis.
- Readers will be encouraged to become involved in the international orphan crisis and challenged to grow in their personal relationship with God.

THE COMPETITION

"Many words rush along like rivers in flood, but deep wisdom flows up from artesian springs." Proverbs 18:4 MSG

Your potential agent or publisher will want to know what other books on the market are similar to your proposed book idea. They want to know that you understand what is already out in the market, and how your book is different.

Below are the steps to complete for this section of your book proposal.

- Start with the title of the comparable book (which is italicized). Type the author, publisher, and year the book was published (all in parentheses).
- Summarize the book in one brief sentence.
- Describe how your book is different (better).

List approximately four to six competing books that are close in nature and genre to your proposed book and recently published (within the last ten years). You can list one older book if it is well known and very similar to your book idea.

An example follows on the next page.

COMPETITION

No books on the market relay the suspense-filled personal account of an American woman fighting a corrupt foreign legal system and her journey to victory as she leans into her sustained faith in God. However, five nonfiction titles portray stories featuring a courageous central female protagonist or have an adoption theme.

    1. *Eat, Pray, Love: One Woman's Search for Everything Across Italy, India and Indonesia* (Elizabeth Gilbert, Viking Adult, February 2006). This book features a woman recovering from a heartbreaking divorce. The author turns to many things through her struggle, but never the one true God as her source of strength during her journey.

    2. *In a Heartbeat: Sharing the Power of Cheerful Giving* (Leigh Anne and Sean Tuohy, Henry Holt and Co., July 2010). Describes a true story of compassion regarding the domestic legal guardianship by a married couple of a young man who attends their children's school, and how their love empowers him to become a famous sport figure. Inspired giving is the main theme, versus faith and miraculous intervention.

    3. *Choosing to See: A Journey of Struggle and Hope* (Mary Beth Chapman with Steven Curtis Chapman, Revell, 2010). Mary Beth Chapman relates her painful journey of living life in the spotlight during the most painful moments of life. Chapman relates the tragic death of her five-year-old adopted daughter and Mary Beth's struggle to heal.

    4. *Orphanology: Awakening to Gospel-Centered Adoption and Orphan Care* (Tony Merida and Rick Morton, New Hope Publishers 2011). This book reveals a number of ways to care for orphans in a biblical perspective and reasons we must. Along with their families' adoption stories, Merida and Morton give steps for action and features on churches doing orphan ministry, faith-based children's homes, orphan hosting groups, and other resources.

5. *Not Without My Daughter* (Betty Mahmoody with William Hoffer, St. Martin's Press, 1987). In August 1984, Michigan housewife Betty Mahmoody accompanies her husband and their four-year-old daughter to her husband's homeland of Iran for a two-week vacation. While visiting the family, her husband reaffirms his fundamental Islam faith and forbids Betty to leave the country with their daughter. This story focuses on Betty's courage in the face of terror and her and her daughter's eventual escape, but it lacks the faith elements of *Until We All Come Home.*

THE AUTHOR

"Do your best to present yourself to God as one approved, a worker who does not need to be ashamed and who correctly handles the word of truth." 2 Timothy 2:15 NIV

This section of the proposal tells why you are qualified to write this book. Make sure the information you share is not overwhelming, but balanced with the proposal as a whole ... about a half page in length.

Start out with your work and other experiences that are connected to the book you are writing. This only needs to be a line or two.

Then talk about your writing experience. List other books, articles, or other pieces you've had published. If you haven't had anything formally published, then list articles in newsletters, church bulletins, etc. where others have read what you wrote.

Describe your social media interaction. Do you have a blog? Are you on Facebook, Twitter, Instagram, etc.? How many people are following you on your various social media outlets?

List your education and training, or anything else that makes you qualified to write.

Next, write a paragraph about your family life (where you live, go to church, etc.). Share a bit about the passion you have about your book's topic/theme.

Give your e-mail address. This is the only section where you talk about yourself and explain to the publisher or agent why you and your book would be a good investment for them.

An example follows on the next page.

THE AUTHOR

Kim de Blecourt is an experienced journalist, adoptive parent and ministry leader with a powerful story of courage and faith in the face of seemingly insurmountable opposition. .

Kim and her husband, Jahn, have been married for thirteen years and are the parents of two children: Jacey (age ten) and their recently adopted son, Jake (age five). They live in Holland, Michigan, where they are members of Immanuel Church. Over the past year, Kim has presented the message of this book through a wide variety of media outlets and at a growing number of speaking venues.

While Kim was in the Ukraine, she was contacted by a casting director from the Oprah Winfrey Network and asked if their team could film her story. However, timing issues could not be worked out. Kim remains committed to telling her story in the most compelling venues possible in order to inspire and educate others.

For more information, visit Kim's ministry website at www.nourishedhearts.com.

THE PROMOTION

"Don't work hard only when your master is watching and then shirk when he isn't looking; work hard and with gladness all the time, as though working for Christ, doing the will of God with all your hearts." Ephesians 6:6–7 TLB

You can't rely on the publishing house or agent to do all the marketing for you. Authors take an active role in the promotion of their books. Many publishers expect their authors to generate at least 50 percent of their book sales. No one can market your book better than you.

How will you get the word out about your book? How do you plan to promote it? This information conveys to the agent or editor that you are committed to actively helping to sell the book. Here are some areas in regards to promotion:

- Endorsements: What important contacts do you have who might be willing to endorse your book? Asking someone who is an expert in the field of your book topic is appropriate. Feel free to ask people you don't know. The worse thing they can say is no. For the proposal, make a list of possibilities.

- Speaking: Are you speaking on the topic of your book at various places? Are you willing to speak more about it? People who've heard you speak will feel like they know you and want to buy your book. Selling books at speaking events is a great way to get the word out about your book.

- Blogging: Blogging creates a built-in audience that will draw the attention of a publisher. To blog means to write articles on a topic that you are interested in that you feel your audience would like. A topic that connects to the book(s) you are writing is best. Many authors hold book contests on their blogs and do interviews on other people's blogs to promote their book. To begin a blog, there are many helps on the Internet. Sites such as Wordpress offer free setup of a blog.

- Writing articles for magazines on the topic, or speaking on television or radio, will also increase your promotional base.

An example follows on the next two pages.

AUTHOR PROMOTION

The author is a media professional and public speaker who will work closely with the publisher to actively promote *Until We All Come Home* through:

- Networks: Focus on the Family, Christian Alliance for Orphans, and other publisher networks
- Regional and national conferences with a focus on adoption, foster care and orphan care, as a speaker
- Live and taped interviews broadcast on Christian and non-Christian television and radio arranged by publisher
- Feature articles published by local newspapers and local and national magazines known to author and publisher
- Feature articles published by leading Christian online ministries known to author and publisher
- *Until We All Come Home* website (nourishedhearts.com), e-promotional strategies, and networking opportunities currently in place.

During her time in Ukraine, Kim de Blecourt continually updated her social network regarding her situation. More than five hundred people followed the story on Facebook, as well as hundreds more through churches and school prayer chains.

Publicity began before Kim and her son, Jake, arrived in the US, including an interview with the local FOX affiliate via Skype on April 21, 2010. (Watch it at http://www.fox17online.com/news/fox17-holland-family-adopting-stuck-in-ukraine,0,2281594.story.)

The author's family homecoming was covered by local FOX and NBC news crews and televised during their 6 p.m., 10 p.m. and 11 p.m. newscasts. (Two of the clips are available at http://www.woodtv.com/dpp/news/local/kent_county/After-1-yr-family-home-with-adopted-son and http://www.fox17online.com/news/fox17-adoptive-mother-holland-volcano-disruptions,0,1446997.story.)

The author's family and their adoption story were featured

in an article by Lorilee Craker in *The Grand Rapids Press*, November 16, 2010, in a story titled, "Adoption Was No Easy Task for Holland Family." (It can be read at http://www.mlive.com/living/grand-rapids/index.ssf/2010/11/adoption_was_no_easy_task_for.html.)

The author was interviewed for a national NPR radio show titled *Snap Judgment* on Friday, January 14, 2010. The interview aired on January 28, 2011 ("One of Our Own," episode 203) and is titled "Not Without My Son." (It is available at http://snapjudgment.org/not-without-my-son.)

THE SUMMARY

"My heart is overflowing with a beautiful thought! I will write a lovely poem to the King, for I am as full of words as the speediest writer pouring out his story." Psalm 45:1 TLB

This section of the book proposal is where you summarize the content of your book. Communicate the full range of the book so the agent or acquisitions editor won't be left wondering whether you can finish the project.

NONFICTION SUMMARY

To summarize your nonfiction manuscript, use a simple outline format. For example:

Chapter 1 – Title of Chapter (if there is one): (Usually begins with the protagonist's name).

Bring out the best points of that chapter in two or three sentences. A good outline will give the publisher or agent confidence in your writing ability, the quality of the book, and its message.

SAMPLE CHAPTERS

For both fiction and nonfiction book proposals, include the first (always the first) two to three chapters (some publishers request the first 50 pages – be sure to know what your agent/publisher requires). If you have a prologue, include it as a chapter. Do not send an introduction. At the end of the summary, type, "Sample chapters follow on pages _____ to _____."

An example follows on the next five pages.

SUMMARY

Endorsements and testimonials: People who were involved with the de Blecourt family during their journey share how the family's story affected their faith.

Foreword: written by a nationally recognized figure regarding the plight of the world's orphans, their importance to the world of tomorrow, and Christians' role in responding to the plight of orphans.

Contents

Prologue

Chapter One: The Crossing, April 18, 2010
Kim and her children flee Ukraine just steps ahead of an angry prosecutor who issued a warrant for Kim's adopted son's return. At the checkpoint out of Ukraine, a border guard announces Kim's arrest. Her two children, who are terrified and waiting alone in a car outside, are left to an uncertain fate.

Chapter Two: First Shades of Gray, May 2009
Jahn and Kim's translator, Boris, asks them to consider a child named Ivan for adoption. Although they feel uncomfortable about their translator involving himself in the adoption process, they select Ivan and spend five days visiting him at the Special Baby Home in Izmail. After days of questioning, they are finally told Ivan is physically and developmentally disabled. During this painful ordeal, an orphanage doctor accuses the de Blecourts of wanting to adopt Ivan to kill him and sell him for body parts. They also tell them that turning back from adopting the child will cause him great emotional harm. In spite of the pain of their decision, the de Blecourts' return to Kiev to begin the process of selecting another child to visit.

Three: The Birth of Fear, May 2009

Just days after the family's return to Kiev, Kim is attacked in broad daylight—struck in the head and nearly knocked unconscious at the top of a wide concrete stairway in Independence Square. Has she been assaulted because she and Jahn did not move ahead to finalize Ivan's adoption? How did her assailant disappear into thin air in a wide expanse of open air? Kim and Jahn share concerns for her safety and wonder whether or not they should choose another child.

Chapter Four: Haunting Faces, June 2009

Kim and Jahn wrestle with fears for their safety as they press ahead to meet two more children—Slavic and Sasha. Each time, their hearts are torn, and Kim becomes more doubtful about not only the process but the safety of their family in a culture where deception is regarded as virtue.

Chapter Five: July Heat, July 2009

In spite of Jahn's fears for Kim's safety, he and Kim make the difficult decision that he must return to Michigan with their daughter, Jacey. But as Kim prepares for her day in court to initiate the adoption of Sasha, she is stopped and threatened by Ukrainian police. Fears for their safety crescendo as Kim prepares for her day in court.

Chapter Six: Winds of Change, August 2009

Kim's hopes of proceeding with a timely adoption are dashed when she receives a devastating appeal notice from a young prosecutor who opposes the adoption of Ukrainian children by foreigners. Her sense of foreboding increases as she questions God's faithfulness in her struggle.

Chapter Seven: Stranded, September 2009

Kim finally receives official custody of Sasha, now legally named Jacob, whom she and Jahn nickname Jake. However, because of the appeal notice, she is still unable to take her new son out of the country. Tension increases as Kim continues to face legal and practical obstacles that threaten not only the goal of bringing Jake home but their physical safety.

Chapter Eight: Echoes of Solitude, October 2009
Kim returns to her own flat, just feet from the police station, and learns the wisdom of hiding in plain sight. In an effort to protect her and her child, she moves her and Jake to a church dormitory and travels to Poland to obtain the Ukrainian visa that will enable her to legally extend her stay in Ukraine.

Chapter Nine: The Advocate, November 2009
Kim meets with her first Ukrainian advocate (attorney). He offers suggestions for her case and relates the discouraging news that it is unlikely that she will prevail. As Kim celebrates Thanksgiving with a group of Americans, she wonders how long she can remain in Ukraine and keep up the fight.

Chapter Ten: Unexpected Gifts, December 2009
Kim and her family are reunited for the Ukrainian holiday celebration, and as the family spends their first Christmas together, their appeal court hearing result is revealed; they must start all over.

Chapter Eleven: The Chill, January 2010
Jahn returns to America alone, leaving Jacey with Kim. Kim is now responsible for the care and safety of two children in a foreign and often hostile culture. Single-handedly, she puts together a new legal team to replace the adoption agency that has abandoned them.

Chapter Twelve: Descending Darkness, February 2010
Kim's faith spirals downward as friends and family prepare for the likely possibility that she will lose her son to the legal process. Kim struggles with depression and defeat but turns to the Word of God as a source of strength.

Chapter Thirteen: Season of Mayhem, March 2010
Following the pre-trial hearing, Kim deals with the angry prosecutor's retribution of putting out a warrant for Jake's return.

She lives in constant fear of being arrested while waiting for her third and final court hearing. During the final court hearing proceedings, she is forced to remain incarcerated in her apartment. But during this time, her faith is strengthened.

Chapter Fourteen: The Paperchase, April 2010
During the post-trial experience, miracle after miracle enables Jake's paperwork to be completed against all odds and in record time. The prosecutor continues his battle against the adoption while Kim manages to legally obtain the necessary paperwork to allow her son to leave Ukraine.

Chapter Fifteen: The Escape, April 2010
Kim escapes from Ukraine with her children in spite of a determined young prosecutor hot on their trail. Iceland's volcano activity forces the grounding of Kim's planes, which leads to her arrest at the Ukrainian border.

Chapter Sixteen: Paradise in Disguise, April 2010
Kim and the children "vacation" in two countries known to be inhospitable to Americans, yet God provides miracles through the kindness of strangers to providentially care for them.

Chapter Seventeen: Until We All Come Home, April 2010
Air travel is still shut down in Europe and threatening Kim's final escape with her children. In yet another act of providence, God provides the protection Kim needs at precisely the right moment, and she and her children arrive home at last to waiting family and friends.

Chapter Eighteen: The Flavor of Family
The dream of family has become reality as Kim describes new life at the de Blecourt home.

Epilogue
Today, the de Blecourt family faces new struggles with adjusting to being home after such an ordeal, but they have found their "new normal" through their faith in God. God has prepared Kim

to share her story through speaking engagements.

Acknowledgment

Recommended Reading

Recommended Resources

SAMPLE CHAPTERS
Sample chapters follow on pages 9 – 40.

FICTION SUMMARY

The summary for a fiction book will demonstrate that you are able to carry the story from beginning to end. It also shows there is enough action throughout the story to keep it interesting. Write the summary in a concise manner. Get to the point. Don't let a lot of flowery words clutter up your descriptions. Write about the main things that happen in the story.

Do not write a chapter-by-chapter outline or use chapter headings. Instead, write a descriptive paragraph for each chapter if you page count per chapter is the standard approximate 10 pages. If you are writing shorter chapters (1-5 pages) which is acceptable for today's reader, then you may want to combine two or three chapters per paragraph. Make sure to include all pertinent details and that it flows as a story summary.

Do not include descriptions in your summary. Just stick to the plot. Here is an example of a fiction summary to review over the next few pages.

FICTION SUMMARY

VALLIKETT'S JOURNEY

Novel based on a true story

Donna D. Flammang as told to Kathy Bruins, Writer

Louis Vallikett's source of supporting his family was gone. Mr. Dole had to sell the farm that Louis worked on to the railroad. Times were hard in the 1870's. A job wasn't easy to find. Fear racked Louis' mind as he tried to figure out what to do to get work. Would he be able to trust God?

The Vallikett family was very close. Louis' wife, Lizzy, was a strong and beautiful woman that he cherished. God blessed them with two daughters, Edith and Louisa, ages 10 and 7. His mother, Bessy, and brother, Will, lived closed by. They also have a much loved dog named Barny. After much discussion and prayer during dinner one night, the family decides to find out more about land in the Dakotas. The fears voiced of Indians, farming conditions, weather, and leaving everything and everybody they knew behind, lead them more to lean on God in their decision and trust him wherever they would go.

Louis and Will go to check out parcels and find out more information for the family to consider. After talking to the claims clerk who said the parcel they were looking at was also being considered by another resident, Louis decides to make the claim. Because of the Homestead Act, they would receive 160 acres of undeveloped land free and clear. They just needed to promise to build a house and reside there for five years. The land that Louis and his family would farm and develop was located on a beautiful lake called Badus Lake.

On the trail, the Valliketts experience challenges from riding for long hours in the wagon, Indians surprising them on the trail, and a storm causing the wagon to overturn. Louis could see that even during those scary times that God was with them.

Upon reaching their destination, they are excited about the possibilities. The community comes to help them build a sod house. In the middle of the night, Indians attempt to steal from them. Louis goes outside to check with his rifle, and is knocked down by the Indian and having the rifle stolen from his hands.

Louis and Will go to town one day to purchase flax seed from Mr. McNeil's store. There they see a drunk, obnoxious and paralyzed Colonel Patch, a man they met on the trail. He has become bitter since an Indian shot an arrow into his spine. They hate seeing their friend like this and God is sought for a solution. Will and Louis find a way to get him to lead training for the community in how to fight Indians.

While Louis and Will are plowing in the fields, they find a different type of stone. They learn it is pipe stone, a material the Indians use to make pipes. Colonel Patch knows a geologist and sends a letter to him to find out what the next step for them is since there is so much on their land.

Winters are hard at Badus Lake. One year roof of the sod house collapses and the family is forced to walk in the freezing temps to Bessy and Will's house. Another year, the town runs out of food and an expedition led by Louis is formed to travel to the next town for supplies.

Will meets Mr. McNeil's daughter, Kacie, who helps out at the store and is the school teacher. They fall in love and decide to marry, but before that happens, a terrible fire consumes several buildings in town and Kacie runs in a building to help some people get out. The roof caves in and she is trapped. Colonel Patch saves her, but dies in the fire. Kacie's recovery is unsure. So a very worried Will stays by her side every day. She may need surgery and may not survive that. She does survive and marries Will.

During the wedding reception a boy delivers a message to Louis. It is from the geologist in Chicago. He wrote that all of the samples were rich with pipestone and that he was sitting on a goldmine. This will bring many jobs to Badus Lake and help the community grow. The challenges of pioneer life lead the Valllikets on a journey of faith where they learn about trusting God. The blessings of God, even with the struggles experienced, shine through in a real and personal way meant to affect the hearts of the characters and the readers.

THE WRITERS' CONFERENCE
SUBMISSION PROCESS

"Let us consider how we may spur one another on toward love and good deeds." Hebrews 10:24 NIV

Attending a writer's conference gives you opportunity to propose your book in person to an agent or acquisitions editor. There are some steps you want to follow in the process that will bring you closer to success. Remember that if a publisher or agent does not accept your book, it doesn't mean you have failed, but you just haven't found the right match yet. Keep trying for one day you will find that place for your manuscript.

Here are some things you can do before, during and after meeting an agent or acquisitions editor:

Before you go to the conference:

- See which agents and acquisitions editors will be at the conference and research them and their companies.
- If allowed, select the people you want to meet with for 15 minutes and register for that meeting.
- Prepare one-sheets to give them when you meet. Also have business cards.
- Practice what you will say about your book. Learn about elevator pitches and have a concise summary about your

book and why you are the person to write it.

During the meeting:

- Be confident. When you approach them, introduce yourself and shake their hand. Give them your business card.
- Let them start the conversation. It will most likely be asking you about your project or you as a writer.
- When the book is asked about, give them your one-sheet and begin to talk about your idea.
- Listen carefully to their advice. Do not argue or defend your work with what they say. They truly are trying to help you.
- If they ask you for a book proposal to be sent to them, take their card for your information. If you are not asked for a proposal, still appreciate the time they have spent with you and the guidance you receive.
- When time is up, don't try to stretch it out for someone else is waiting to meet with them. Shake their hand again and thank them for meeting with you.

After the meeting:

- Review the information said to you and jot notes so you won't forget.
- Write them a "thank you" note to send after the conference.

THE ONE-SHEET

A one-sheet is a condensed, one-page version of your book proposal. One-sheets are also referred to as sell sheets or pitch sheets.

Put the following information on your one-sheet:

- your name and contact information
- book title
- an image that reflects your book
- pitch
- back-cover copy
- genre
- word count
- author photo and bio

The order in which you present this information is your choice. An example of a one-sheet is on the following page. The example would be all on one page.

Kathy Bruins
Christian Author/Speaker
(address)

(phone)
(e-mail)
(website)

Vallikett's Journey

Little House on the Prairie meets *Lonesome Dove*

Losing faith and finding it in the hard places in life.

In the mid-1800's in St. James, Minnesota, Louis Vallikett had to go home and tell his wife the terrible news that he'd lost his job—again—and didn't know how he was going to support his family. After some discussions, he and his wife, Lizzy, decide to register for a homestead in the Dakotas … an untamed land that could bring joy or grief.

Louis and Lizzy, with their daughters, Edith and Louisa, and Louis's mother and brother, join a wagon train. The two-week journey entails terrifying events that test the strength of each of them.

When they reach Badus Lake, Louis struggles to get past his disappointment in life and to rely on God. The Vallikett family has times of laughter and tears as Louis learns the value of family and being a good neighbor.

Historical-inspired manuscript of approximately 50,000 words.

Author * Speaker * Dramatist
Kathy Bruins believes everyone has a story to tell. She walks with her clients who have a story to tell. Kathy is hired to tell their stories through her writing. Her upcoming release is *Exposing the*

Darkness: From a Small Town Where People Don't Talk or Tell, written with Malynda Osantowski, a survivor of sex trafficking. Other books include *A Season of God's Daily Influence.* Her speaking topics cover teachings from the Bible, writing, drama, and cancer.

For more information, please visit www.kathybruins.com.

THE NON-CONFERENCE

SUBMISSION PROCESS

Attending a writers' conference where you can meet agents and acquisitions editors' face-to-face is the best opportunity for pitching your book idea.

If you cannot attend a writers' conference, you can still submit your proposal to an acquisitions editor or agent. First, pray about which publishing house or agent to submit to. Ask God for direction as you research publishers and agents who work with the genre of your book.

The non-conference submission process is as follows:

First, create the list of agents and/or acquisition editors to whom you want to submit. The *Writer's Market* and *The Christian Writer's Market Guide* are excellent sources to use when you create your submission list. Agents and acquisition editors that work with the kind of book you're writing. Verify the information by visiting the agents' and acquisition editors' websites (things change quickly in the publishing business.) Address your query letter (queries will be explained in an upcoming chapter) to the appropriate person. Make sure the name is spelled correctly. Find out the submission guidelines for each publisher or agent you are considering. Some want proposals mailed, while others prefer e-mail submissions.

If you're sending a proposal by mail, print it out on plain white paper. Do not three-hole punch, staple, or paperclip the pages together. You may use a rubber band to keep them together. If you would like to receive a response right away indicating they received it, include a stamped, self-addressed postcard they can easily drop in the mail. If the guidelines indicate they accept certified mail, use that—the post office will send you an Electronic Return Receipt upon delivery. If you would like to get your manuscript back if it's rejected, include a self-addressed envelope with enough postage to cover the pages.

If multiple submissions are allowed in the guidelines, you may send your manuscript to several publishers and/or agents at the same time. But let them know in your cover letter that you are sending multiple submissions.

After you have mailed out your proposal, get started on another project. Instead of just sitting and waiting for a response, keep your mind active on other work. If you have heard no response within a month, you may contact them preferably by email to see if they received it. Don't ask any other questions than that. Do not call them by phone.

If you get a rejection, don't be discouraged. If you could wallpaper your house with all the rejections you've may receive, you may need to take a different angle. But a few rejections probably just means you haven't sent the manuscript to the right place yet. Acquisitions editors and agents rarely have the time to write notes to authors with advice on improvement. If you do receive feedback, consider the suggestions seriously. You can learn a lot from them.

THE QUERY LETTER

If you are unable to attend a writers' conference, you can introduce yourself and your book to a publisher or agent with a query letter. The publisher's writers' guidelines will indicate whether a query letter is to be sent before submitting a proposal and/or the complete manuscript. If you send a proposal or manuscript, the letter you send is a cover letter.

At the beginning of a query letter, type the date, the name of the agent or editor, the name of the organization, and their address (all spelled correctly). In the salutation, address the letter to the contact using formal names such as Mr. or Ms. Jones. The first paragraph of the body of the letter needs to draw him or her in so they want to read more. Start out with a question or statement that will grab their attention.

For a nonfiction book, talk about why the story or information is important to readers. Explain the take-away.

For a fiction book, the first two or three paragraphs should give the agent/editor an idea about the content of your story. What conflict is the main character experiencing? What are the possible options for overcoming the obstacles to their goal?

In the next line, give the title of the book, the genre, status, and word count.

The final paragraph contains information about your skills

and experience in writing along with a little bit about you personally.

Indicate what you have enclosed with the letter (if anything), and thank them for their consideration.

Query letters need to be one page long, in Times New Roman 12-point font, with one-inch margins all around.

An example of a query letter can be found on the next page.

(date)

(name of editor)
(company)
(address)

Dear (surname of editor):

Prayer ministry is fast-growing in churches today. Being equipped to lead any position is essential for success. I have a passion for this helping people to learn about prayer along with teaching leaders. *Prayer Leader: Inside and Out* focuses on the spiritual building of a prayer leader, and how he or she can discover God's plan for them in His Kingdom work.

Being a prayer leader for the past four years, and then becoming the denomination's first prayer leader this year in my city, I have learned a lot about the development of the organization and as a leader. With my twenty years of experience in ministry leadership, I can help others who are passionate about this ministry. This book will also serve to help leaders stay encouraged and serve with perseverance.

I am also a team member of the Great Lakes Regional Synod H.O.P.E. (Houses of Prayer Equipping) Team. I have a bachelor's degree in religious education. Enclosed is my writing résumé for your convenience.

The projected length of my book is approximately 150 to 200 pages, and estimated completion date of the manuscript is January of 2016.

If you have any questions, please contact me at (contact information).

Sincerely,
Kathy Bruins

CONCLUSION

"Don't burn out; keep yourselves fueled and aflame. Be alert servants of the Master, cheerfully expectant. Don't quit in hard times; pray all the harder. Help needy Christians; be inventive in hospitality." Romans 12:11–13 MSG

We hope the material covered in this book has been helpful to you and that we have relieved your fear of creating a book proposal.

God has a wonderful purpose for you in writing your book. Consider the words of the psalmist in Psalm 45:1 NIV: "My heart is stirred by a noble theme as I recite my verses for the king; my tongue is the pen of a skillful writer." For thousands of years, God has used writers to spread His good message, and He still does that today. Even if your book would not be labeled as Christian, you serve a gracious God who inspires your writing. The work of our hands bring the Lord honor and glory in all we do.

We wish you blessings in the writing adventure God has you on!

Do you not know?

Have you not heard?

The Lord is the everlasting God,

the Creator of the ends of the earth.

He will not grow tired or weary,

and his understanding no one can fathom.

He gives strength to the weary

and increases the power of the weak.

Even youths grow tired and weary,

and young men stumble and fall;

but those who hope in the Lord

will renew their strength.

They will soar on wings like eagles;

they will run and not grow weary,

they will walk and not be faint.

Isaiah 40:28–31 NIV

BOOK PROPOSAL TEMPLATE

You can use our Book Proposal Template by filling in the blanks with your information and printing out the pages. Just type in this link:

http://kathybruins.com/book-proposal-files/

A zip file will download, which you can open to retrieve the template files. The blank files have headers to guide you, but wherever you see "(Delete)," make sure to delete that header.

If you have problems or questions regarding the template, please contact **author@kathybruins.com.**

72898892R00035

Made in the USA
Middletown, DE
09 May 2018